D1387587

Will and Kate's
Big Fat Gypsy Wedding

Will and Kate's Big Fat Gypsy Wedding

Alex and Rory

SIMON &
SCHUSTER

London · New York · Sydney · Toronto

A CBS COMPANY

First published in Great Britain in 2011 by Simon & Schuster UK Ltd
A CBS COMPANY

1 3 5 7 9 10 8 6 4 2

Simon & Schuster UK Ltd
1st Floor
222 Gray's Inn Road
London, WC1X 8HB

www.simonandschuster.co.uk

Simon & Schuster Australia
Sydney

The publishers have made every effort to contact those holding rights in the material
reproduced in this book. Where this has not been possible, the publishers will be
glad to hear from those who recognise their material.

A CIP catalogue copy for this book is available
from the British Library.

ISBN: 978-0-85720-762-3

Printed and bound in Italy by LEGO SpA

Contents

A Royal Welcome from Wills and Kate

Wills: Oh, hey there. Look, thanks soooo much for picking this book up. It really means a lot to me and Kate that people are interested in our wedding and want to discover more about our Traveller origins, like. This book is a celebration of our blissful union but I also hope it helps to show that Travellers isn't all bad people at the end of the day. We aren't a load of tax dodgers (Nanny stopped that years ago), we aren't thieves (well, perhaps me Uncle Andy is), and we aren't lazy (we want to work but we aren't allowed to for security reasons. Okay?!)
 Anyway, read on and see what things are really like behind the scenes of a wedding in one of the world's most secretive communities. Oh, Kate wants to say something . . .

Kate: I hope you rahlly enjoy these pages and that!

Build-up to the
Big Day

Pavin' the Way for a Wedding

Wills: Tarmackin' Horseguards ahead of the wedding and linin' our pockets as we do. We also run a good line in scrap metal and the like.

Monarch of the Hen

Kate: Bea, me, Mummy, and Genie – just before things got well lively on the dance floors of Slough! (Unfairly, we would later be ordered to leave the city centre.)

Bare-knuckle Fisticuffs

Harry: Polo is an EPIC rush but it doesn't match the buzz I get from a proper car-park beef! This was really just a great stag do all round.

A National Event

Kate: Sadly, in the wake of the wedding announcement a certain element began to peddle black-market memorabilia.

7

Drama Queen

Wills: Nana got proper aggro about all the wedding arrangements . . .
Charles: 'Mother, please, not the face!'

The Lord Chamberlain is commanded

by The Queen to invite

. . . .

to Will and Kate's Big Fat Gypsy Wedding

at Westminster Abbey

on Friday, 29th April, 2011 at 11.00 a.m., or thereabouts

Dress: Ladies in 'exotic fairy tale' attire

Gentlemen in sleeveless shirts

Horses and dogs can be tethered on College Green

No fighting inside the venue — please use the car park provided

How it All Began

How to 'Grab' Yourself a Princess

Wills: Gosh you looked fit the night we met, Babes. Sorry about grabbing you like that, what?

Kate: Oh, you mustn't be sorry darling! Why that's just gypsies' ways, innit?

CLARENCE HOUSE
LONDON SW1A 1BA

15th November 2010

Dearest Darling Kate,

I have been doin' my head, like, trying to write this! I am bereft of words but suffice it to say I think you are proper, proper mint. Like a thief in the night you stole my breath when we met at the fashion show and I haven't caught it since — perhaps that's why I am struggling to say what I feel now! (Or maybe it's because of that bottle of White Lightning I quaffed last night at the Nigerian embassy do.) Anyhow, here goes...

Catherine Elizabeth Middleton, will you marry me?! All I ask in return for making you my Princess is that you give up your job to cook and clean for me and don't go out without either me or your father escorting you ever again...

Say 'Yes' woman!
Wills

Right Royally In Love!

Our Engagement Photo

Kate: The dove looks proper mint, dont'cha think?!

Wills: The guy what done the photo is one of the best. (Quite rightly Wedgwood are turning this into a plate.)

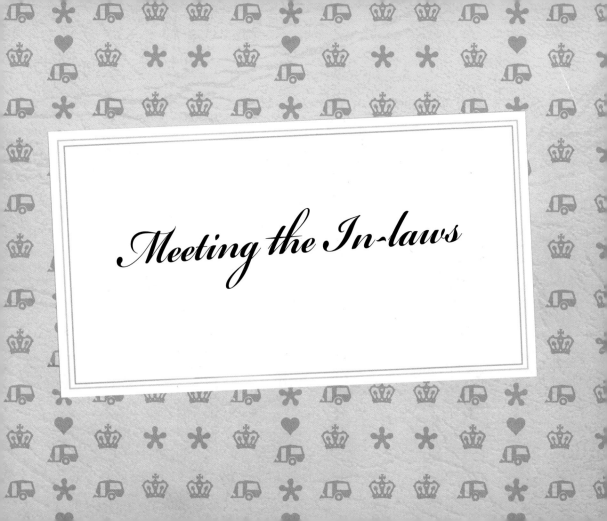

Meeting the In-laws

A Proud and Honourable People

Phil: You see dis ink on me arm? Dis means tradition, don't you know? . . . So now I've telled yer, clear off me site!

The Gypsy King (and Queens)

Wills: Me Great Nan and Great Aunt having a dance and that while Grand Papa plays a few licks on the guitar. You'd never have guessed there was a war on!

'The Gypsy Olympics', Appleby 2010

Wills: Zara winning gold in the 'Driving at an unsafe speed through a built-up area' event. The judges said she showed 'almost total disregard for other road users'. Gosh we're proud.

From Egg-Chaser to Horse-Racer

Kate: Zara's fiancé doing his bit in the Man vs. Horse event.

Wills: To be sure a lot of chaps would look down on racing against a horse but Tinders gave it everything . . . and won massive banter points for it.

A 'Special Trade' Representative

Andy: 'It is with great honour and as a show of respect for our two proud cultures that I convey to you this precious heirloom. Now, fellas, can I interest you in 20ft of copper wiring?'

Prejudice

NOTICE OF EVICTION

FAO:

The House of Windsor (ex Saxe-Coburg and Gotha)

And the House of Schleswig-Holstein-Sonderburg-Glücksburg

Balmoral Castle Estate

Royal Deeside, Aberdeenshire, Scotland

In the County Court of Aberdeenshire
Case No: 9GUCB2141RS
Warrant No: X0000XXX99
Issue Date: 13th August 2009

AS A CONSEQUENCE OF YOUR *GROSS DESPOILING OF AN AREA OF OUTSTANDING BEAUTY* YOU WILL BE EVICTED IF YOU HAVE NOT VACATED THE ABOVE SITE BY:
4PM ON AUGUST 19TH 2009

Claimants: National Trust for Places of Historic Interest or Natural Beauty
Solicitors: Nutten Caulfeld

Aberdeenshire County Court

CERTIFIED

22

Throne Out!

Wills: (*Opposite page*) The eviction notice served us in 2009 and (*above*) Balmoral as it was after we moved our caravan site on to Kensington Palace.

'Why Don't You Go Back to Germany?!'
Wills: Nan doing one after the opening of Parliament turned into a right show.

Our Big Fat Royal Gypsy Wedding!

Looking Like a Princess Already . . .
Kate: Ahhhh, 22 stone of highly flammable, bank-breaking, thigh-scarring joy!

. . . and Feeling Maid-up!

Kate: With my darling sister, Pipps, and also Shannon and Aileen (whose faces have had to be blurred for legal reasons).

In celebration of Wills and Kate
April 29, 2011 – Wedding Reception

Champagne toast

Fag Break

To eat:
'Iceland Party Pack' – An exquisite selection of canapés showcasing
the best cuisine from around the world
To drink:
Assorted soft drinks and a range of alcoholic beverages* (snakebite on request)

The speeches

There will then be a short dog-fighting display led by the Archbishop of Canterbury

Carriages 4am**

*Available only for men and married women
**Please respect our neighbours by doing your 'grabbing' as quietly as possible!

Invitation-only

Kate: Unfortunately we just weren't able to accommodate everyone on the day.

Rock 'N Royal
Wills: Hazza letting his heir down at the Wedding party with Chelsy!

Abbey + Bling = Party!

Wills: A historic moment.

Kate: Yeh, we knew the cake was big and that but to be told we'd smashed the record for height *and* weight was a fairytale, like!

31

Home Sweet Home

Wills: Kate and I chose the wild, unspoilt beauty of North Wales as the site of our marital caravan.

The landscape is simply breathtaking . . . and also we've managed to run a cable off next door's satellite dish.